HOW I JOINED HUMANITY AT LAST

How I Joined Humanity at Last

DAVID ZIEROTH

HARBOUR PUBLISHING

Published by
HARBOUR PUBLISHING
P.O. Box 219
Madeira Park, BC Canada V0N 2H0

We acknowledge the financial support of the Government of
Canada through the Book Publishing Industry Development
Program and the Province of British Columbia through the
British Columbia Arts Council for our publishing activities.

Front cover painting by David Zieroth

Canadian Cataloguing in Publication Data

Zieroth, Dale
  How I joined humanity at last

  Poems.
  ISBN 1-55017-182-8

  I. Title.
PS8599.I47H68 1998   C811'.54   C98-910236-X
PR9199.3.Z53H68 1998

THE CANADA COUNCIL | LE CONSEIL DES ARTS
FOR THE ARTS | DU CANADA
SINCE 1957 | DEPUIS 1957

This book is for the Saturday night group,
who heard the poems first,

and for Laura and Marjalena.

DAVID DALE

Forced to abandon him
by a grade one teacher who could not accept
two boys with the same name, I accepted
my second. I think of David
as a skin dropped, a ball
lost in the summer grass.

My parents often spoke of him
or mouthed my new name
as if I were a guest
and they were waiting politely
for his return

because what faults I had
could never spring from him.
Well, did he grow up
through change, embarrassment,
and try to speak the lines
reserved after all for him? He never did.

When I meet him now
at dawn or just before sleep, he stands
speechless although I know he wants from me
more than words.

Lately, when I cut myself
on paper and the sharp red line wells over
and falls, his young mouth
is pressed against my hand.

(1991)

CONTENTS

PART III:

PART I

WHAT HE OWNS

… owns him
when objects break down.
The alternator in the car
dead now, modern junk
he must pay his mechanic to extract
and replace.

The old Volvo at least
did not die on the freeway but chose
a lane close to home to blink its lights
at him, dashboard growing dim.
He has been stranded before,
in former lives.
He sits again,
his rage nicely controlled;
no point fuming
at metal, the factory flaw,
the nation-state he glides through
(mostly) cushioned
against every bump and dive.

Out of India, millennia ago, he first
moved, wanting to own
where he stood,
but a neighbour had already claimed
where he was—and so he sprawled
over passes, oceans
until every bit of earth
was accounted for, written up
in legal plots and lots.
He steps out of his car now, closes the door,
automatically locking it,
and begins to walk.

THE ROBINS

for J.A.

"He sometimes felt himself to be training for an
undisclosed event; he expected change—he had
no clear idea of what kind—or perhaps even
upheaval, and he was on the lookout for the first
signs, the first small indication that his life was
about to be transformed."
—Ian McEwan, *The Child in Time*

For one month the robins fought
in the trees outside his windows
as they had when he lived
in the house on 23rd,
the apartment before that,
at the co-op and now here.
For this month they threw spiky
challenges over prime territory,
the trees he happened to live near.
Each male wanted control
over these lush evergreens.
The nest of the previous victor
had not increased their numbers; instead
the comings and goings of the adults
suddenly ceased.

Perhaps a squirrel
spotted the droppings and zeroed
in. Or the damp inner rot of the shade
kept the eggs from the final conquering
warmth of the mother. No doubt
the tree was involved somehow.
For a month he heard screaming
if not from the rage of the robins
then from the gulls

scooping in from the harbour
to cruise the roads and parks.
The black spirit of crows
cut through his air space
on its path to the kill.
Tiny kinglets in the firs
moved ten thousand times a day.

FUNCTION OF THE INDIVIDUAL

The function of the individual
he realizes as he travels through town
is to provide the lightning strike
to matter.
What God once did in beautiful
biblical illustrations
he now must do.
The waterfront, for instance,
must be charged up, revved higher
until, incandescent, it shimmers and soothes
the men and women
who stumble mornings
out of the Seabus
and into time.

Loathsome are some of those bodies.
But he sees them now
as uncharged lumps
unable to grip
the time they have in this
configuration of weary mouth and heavy plunging step.
Up the escalator he rides with them,
careful not to stand in front
of those who wander
with their demons.
The cruise ship out the window
has arrived at dawn
and now from its white sides
happy angels watch and watch
and are ignored in turn.

All travellers move time
aside as they go, and as they pass by
it changes, collects, leaps ahead again

so each travels through
what has been shucked off
and waits patiently
for the lightning eye to burn it up
to the cloudy thin-cloudy sky seen in the sea,
in the harbour's oil and white wave.

FATHER'S WORK

When he was home,
he was absent. And yet
several summers now dead,
he still sends love
back over that line
I've kept alive for him
in the far western
corner of a thought and along which
I will someday also vanish.

So it was work he fled to:
he pulled animals off one another
when they fought and tangled.
He killed and emptied the pig
and set in motion my
imagination: beside the wet entrails
the rocks on the ground shone,
colourful intestines
I called gut-stones
and for years half believed
a father's force
turned flesh directly into gems.

I myself go to an office, a room,
but he went outside, machines
needing a patch or thrust
into flame.
Now I'd take his hand,
lead him to a table
where my children spread paintings,
and ask him to contemplate
men and women who seem always
to be striking off the page.
Where are they going, I ask.

Where can I intercept them
and get them to rest?

I reach for more tasks
to help avoid
the unpleasantness that rises
sometimes from leisure
—and I think of his Sunday:
he reached out and made stillness,
urged animal and family
to join in reflecting
the moment a soul
once born is born again.
Wife, sons, horse, dog,
the claw of the hammer,
the blade of the scythe
thus prepared for Monday,
its arc upward into the long life
I'm pushing through right now,
both far and not far from
the nights we sank and never moved,
brothers with the stones
appearing in the moonlit fields
after each passing
of our father's plough.

MY MOTHER'S WAIL

When guests first came to our house
—young women destined to wed
into our family—we warned them
Mum might wail in the part of the night
when we had no chance to hold off
what drifted through the house,
up the stairs to the beds where
we lay, suddenly awake, our hearts
ringing up our brains
frozen by her long vowel
—uuu—unformed by tongue
as it came straight up from
inside my mother where we didn't
think anyone ever lived.

Next morning we joked, and Mother
laughed, no longer embarrassed,
for she herself had never heard
the ur-sound she made, had only
once or twice caught a little
of its end when Dad rolled close
and shook her back to us. He said
we should record her
and make a bundle, and once,
I planned to go to her when next
that moan rolled from her slack mouth,
to comfort her as she would surely
comfort me, but when the time came
I did not, could not, for fear
that who I heard would wake
and be someone other than my mum.

Sometimes I see her
flannel nightgown on the stairs

and in her arms extra blankets for
the night. She tucks in all who
shelter under her roof, she stokes
the fire last, checks
doors, glances in on sleeping forms,
sends her prayers up through
rafters and on to the stars
and then settles with
her dark and starts the roving
back through day and week;
and year after year the speed
of moving becomes a falling
in which she cries out for us.

There seems to be no gene for wailing
passed on to us, no
nightly crying out of our miserable selves
to frighten those around us,
and yet I fear some sound
out of us so low as to be
below the normal pitch of voice,
toneless ululating
close to the beginning
of sound that keeps with it
a realm I never could
imagine by daylight though in the dark
I saw too well what halts and waits
inside my mother's shell.

GOODBYE TO DAUGHTER

This isn't goodbye of the kind
you'd expect to read as a stat
in some tabloid column, some semi-serious
exposé on fathers and their failures
to keep one hand steady
in the family, pounding out a blessing,
while the other marches down the page
underlining, ticking, drifting sideways
to lift a cup that says
"Dad's the Greatest."

This goodbye happens every morning.
I knock and then enter,
find her dreaming,
put my cheek
next to hers and we murmur.
I slip down the stairs,
recall worry like a stick
that stirred up anger, our arrangement
to leave the hall light on
so when she comes in late
(from where I can't ask)
the darkness signals
and my heart jumps
and remembers

my father died
and my mother hurried
to step into his grave
months later. I thought never to cross
that kind of line again—going helpless
to the world;
I place myself where work
can be done and un-done

and done right, in the office,
safe from such news
that would shred my plans
and push me
to repeat what can only be held
and held
and never said.

OFFICE ENCHANTER

I want a lateral transfer
into the position of office enchanter.
Think of the power
I'll add to my workload;
what's the point of working here
if I can't control change?
Two problems immediately
arise: I'm not tall enough
to lock into the eyes
of those who look up
and thus maintain
the force of my glow—plus

I don't have hands scabby enough
to hang out the white sleeves.
But men of any size, shape or smell
command; it could be done.
The other problem is perhaps
the greater: the position
is not yet vacant,
the incumbent strides by
haranguing reason
we find no fault with
when we gather later to spit
his words from our tongues.

Suddenly I have to ask
why I want his wattle-skin.
Wouldn't office allies
feel at first too much
vertigo in switching
to my particular good?
Also, it's never lateral.
But give me a chance

and you won't sweat his way again.
Under my spell, you would willingly
volunteer for work formerly vilified,
give up the photocopier,

and go home rested—to dream
of the new bosom: my office
where I urge each
to combine all talents
in the search for
—and creation of—
the community of hours,
the nakedness of equality
no sore individual could punch through
back into this sad
inadequate criss-crossed
state our present enchanter
wants us to kiss.

MEMO TO MYSELF

If this committee is going to build
between what it is mandated to do
and what we can reasonably agree upon,
we had better meet more often:
in the morning, say, or
with our children as they cluster
at the swings, fighting for space
next to the favoured of the day.
But now out of us
rises distaste for one voice
whose words leave me fuming—later—
because at the time

he smiled shyly enough
to give the feeling he, too,
was a bit unsure of his position
on the thorny matter of money,
of need and desire—for all committees
deal in desire, he says, and I should remember
I am after all only one chemical
in the group. He says if we could
please open our folders

we should find there the figures
and yellow paper where once before
we committed our former selves
—but I also see colleagues
place paper up to their faces, blank
masks to wear
now and through to the end
so he who seeks control cannot be seen.
We are guided only
by the spoken word—it arcs across the table
and lands and penetrates

the soft, embracing ear. This deafness
of members one to another, I must remind
myself, we have all created
and will need to live with
until we meet again.

SLEEPS AND DREAMS

All night I rise between dreams
to nibble at the half-light,
then sink down, reassured
I am not yet lost,
still in a body
that hurls down halls
all day. Now and then
I turn my head to find
another part of the pillow,
a cool patch for my sweat.

Around my bed as I surface
I glimpse my colleagues
who come, apparently,
to spend the night observing
how I stuff the quilt
between my knees.
They've heard my complaints
about rising up
into the face they count upon
—and they want to see for themselves
the effort I claim to make.

I've told them all
the way down can be slow, hard,
flagstones far apart, no rules
or manuals to help
get on with it; they don't believe
I'd enter work without a mandate,
but I tell them
no one argues here,
argument's for paper and file
and isn't a mode that works,
and once my head is down,

the body stills, the eyes
race beneath lids into
a black bear, a glove,
a lost father sailing by.

I can't say I like this work exactly
but it, too, must be done—
and it does have rewards:
no preparation required or even
possible, no quick pre-meetings;
I never drift off or imagine
what the speaker looks like
without clothes—in fact
there is no speaker;
nor does information travel down
from the top dogs in management—
there is no management,
there is no top; I never
drive through drizzle
to reach this work; rather
it comes to me, greets me
with visions and frights
I worry through
next day, wearing the half-smile
my colleagues comment on,
sure I've discovered a way
into primal schemes
they have no guard against.

TEACHING THE COMMA

I'm teaching but this time
it's not the problem of noisy students
or poor preparation; this time
I'm teaching in a dress shop,
discussing the comma
when customers drift in
to lift bright cottons.
I keep up my lecture, soon
little more than prattle.
My female students throw off
winter duds and hold up
spring fashions to one another.
The young men pull down their
caps; they know I'm a stickler
and soon I'll blow.
I illustrate what links
and what breaks, how little marks
on paper mean because they tell us
where to stop and when to go and
how to breathe our way through matters
of weight. Then in she comes, she's
suddenly among us, running her fingers
along the desks, twirling through
the racks, dropping her bag
on my notes, pivoting over the lectern.
All commerce stops;
the distant din of cash dies down
in envy that this woman
is so bold to tackle me. I feel
my hackles rise, and yet I love
what she has done: drawn everyone
here and now to focus. We see
her delicate glamour, the careful
marks upon her face that say

beauty is an exercise only half of us
get right. I am sorely tempted to
roar and spout but instead invite her
loveliness to speak, to open her
lucky youthfulness to words,
to test (for her own sake of course)
everything else she might be.

PHILOSOPHY

I'm rushing up institutional
steps wide enough to take
an auditorium full of wits
just recently gestured to
by an old professor draped
in crepe, his head so full
of Kant it fairly droops.
Now it's my turn, to teach
the incoming crowd, but
I am flying to an office
on another level to find, I think,
the right book—when I discover
my pants are missing, I have
no pants, I have only
the usual Jockey underwear, regulation
black for philosophy instructors.

Something tells me immediately
to keep running, to run right up
the stairs to the last
fire exit and get on the roof,
find there a discarded wing
that I could use to cover
my unusualness or perhaps to fly
past the undergraduates
as they wait by large doors to enter
my lecture on the meaning of self
in modern times, how it never
seems quite to be our own
but something parallel, running
nakedly alongside and making faces
we can't ignore no matter
how much we reason and divide.

Instead I continue charging
up and down the stairs, startling
from time to time a secretary
but meeting no other
who could supply me with either pants
or answers,
and puffing, I sit down
and contemplate my long legs, the beauty
of the kneecap, the calf, the ankle
and the arch—and then
rise up on tiptoes and walk back
and enter the auditorium.

CONSIDER THE MEN

We lock ourselves into days
when nothing gets done but sweat
and not the good kind; but then
how extravagantly we dream, toss all
our saved holiday lives into the car
and roll away, our cigarette smoke
sailing out the window one last time.
Now we're going pure
for two weeks, find ourselves suddenly
up against the kids who seem
only to be talking to their mother
—and I'll admit I'm half
on the tasks left behind,
counting phone booths along the way.

And then returning to the office:
that's the glory-be, to have gone
and felt the summer unravel
out of my feet, to nap while the green
grows up through my chair, sip
the drinks that appear
near my still-white hand,
the same one that grips again
my friend the desk, its broad fake top
waiting for arrangement, the in, the out,
the top drawer where the clips
are kept, the pens, the pills,
the comfort of the lists.

THE PRESENTATION

In a community meeting such as this
we who are loyal to the concept
crowd the back rows while Mr and Mrs
Antagonized commandeer
the front rows, fill space
with their friends, and soon
begin shouting questions at the
man up front, the presenter, him
with the pastel suit who is telling them
change in their lives has arrived.
I respect vehemence in any form

so I turn on my hard seat in the hall
to investigate my own resolve,
which I'm surprised to say
is rapidly waning. I cast
nervous smiles at my friends
gathered in the row behind,
and we share knowing glances
although what exactly leaps between us
can only be decided later, in our own
meeting when we wrangle
through meaning in this event
(Was it change versus no change,
their change versus ours?)
and at this point

I rise to leave but find
I am opening my mouth instead. I am
about to speak and can't recall
what I intended to say.
Dear friends at the back,
tilt your ears to me,
dear Mr and Mrs A.,

by tomorrow or deep in the week
it may not matter if my words
ring with reason, but now
and for fifteen seconds
both back row and front have paused
to hear what comes out of me.

THE SHADOW MEETING

After we have met and talked,
we meet and talk again
in a different way. Earlier
we worked at consensus,
urged one another in and out
of corners, stances, disputations
until we could go on
no longer without flying from
our agenda into disarray.
But now away from file

folders safely tucked in cars
or under arms, I discover
how outside the night air
does not appear in the minutes
but starts nevertheless to shadow
the previous work, to un-work
and let fly feelings unacceptable
at the table. And having left

to travel home
and begin to write up
the next step, we leave behind
forms of bent intensity at the table,
and forms outside, standing at the edge
of the rain, mildly laughing;
these parking lot
loyalties and longevities
rewrite and revise
what all agree did perhaps occur
before we drift off one by one,
dark collar pulled up
to turn the white face
into night.

FOOT RUB

After the bath and the story,
after the mother has left for the night,
the father comes with his hands
and takes up the child's feet.
His thumbs smooth along the arch
of the first foot, across
the pad below the toes
where more than ever
the flesh is waiting for touch.
Up the ankle, along the thin limbs,
squeezing down
to the Achilles' heel where the day
has locked itself in and must now
be eased, so that the feet
can finally stop kicking dust.

This daughter is fond of saying
she has four feet
so he must rub twice on each foot
the wrinkled pink lines given her
before birth. Soft, tiny,
the last to drop from the womb
yet which now carry her
over stones. The father
feels the child change, relax, stare,
set off on a dream-journey
he cannot follow.

An old friend once said
toxins are released through the feet
—and so he goes next to wash his hands.
He turns the soap over and over
without a thought. He shakes drops
into the sink and towels dry.

The hurts and poisons
of his youngest child he does not
keep unto himself but lets drain
away in his own hurry
for the evening's peace.

SPELLING

Because there are words he does not want
his youngest child to hear in conversation,
he spells them out:
"i-c-e c-r-e-a-m"
and "k-i-l-l-i-n-g." The child aches
to know, and guesses, lunges at the context,
not yet knowing adults talk
of a body found in the park nearby
as their way of keeping
dismemberment in the city
outside.

He knows words not given up to the air
may live inside him,
and he needs the peace that comes
with talk, with sharing
what can only be whispered
or spelled out. The child
hears letters tumble down to her
and she grasps at them, a vowel
or a hard sound.
Do these letters from her father
wait for her at night, accumulate
below her window,
coalesce at the level of her door

while he sleeps and cannot hear
what she spells out, her mouth
the perfect O-letter
she is trying to send up the stairs
past the failure of the night-light
into the alpha brain
of her protector,
into his fetal shape

itself now without the logic of a-b-c
so much needed to manoeuvre
out of the dark.

LIVING SUCCESS

After an Elvis sighting
in a nearby mall,
the members of our committee
were more alert
as if they looked into each other
and saw beneath the death wish
a love to waft us all
high above our culture. That day,

fast and sure
in our pace, decisions
were love songs
to slip into and improvise
until harmonies led the way.
We struck up alliances,
we learned to read glances,
we set aside gradation
and glowed the kind of glow

that gets work done. But afterward
I found myself staring down again
into my personal flops (tiredness
that clogs, lack of will that chokes),
errors done and continued,
unable to shut down
voices likely enough to stick to me,
not always singing. In such moods
rock 'n' roll makes me weep
and wail, stuck here in my lonesome craving
easy enough to mock;
and in the moment I press
a hand to my head, does it matter
I mastered earlier that day
a certain form

and presented it to my peers
who saw me then as the one and only,
perfect tone and key?

PEOPLE I MEET WITH MEET WITH ME

None of them
has the face of an ambulance driver,
but what did you expect?
Each of my colleagues,
like me, has a long list
of sensitivities, and together
we work by moving
from nuance to nuance,
carrying on through connotation alone;
no face of a salesman

who wants to win you over
to his fabulous merchandise,
his plan. Yet someone sells me
shy and winsome glances
until I have no integrity left;
I'm caving in
so fast, accepting ideas
not my own and swaying
under a most reasonable wand.
I am a pawn, one of the quiet ones
waiting to be moved,

doodling on my agenda,
disguised as one who mulls over,
who raises his hand after checking to see
who else has raised a hand,
a pack-person,
a conduit for others,
that which is needed to bounce
against but which at the moment
has no bounce itself, unable to initiate,
barely able to pretend.

WHEN WE FIRST FELT OUR MINDS

When we felt our minds pull away
from the natural world, we formed
a committee to study
such separation from wing and wave,
lung and liver. Then
far beyond ourselves,
we grew weary and soon discovered
(or perhaps invented)
an enduring interest
in each other.
So here I am again, elbows
on the table, briefcase gaping

on the floor. A new member
has joined us, and soon
she will overcome initial shock
and speak. How long before she
honours our mistakes; and will she
joke and act the clown,
hold up documents pointedly
from the past as if to say
she has found a totem at last?
We find instead
organizational visions
we wish to project onto others,
now we see the subject
is always us, the few and the many.
A heart leaps to the table,

demands my thinking admit a wild red
turning. I take it up
as it slides among the files
along a path, perhaps my own.
Will the eyes of my colleagues clear,

their hands turn soft in this room
where our bodies wait
until the talk turns down,
for only then can they
rise from their wooden places,
stretch and leave.

THE GOOD DAY

That the sun shines
and I can feel
on my skin its clean burst
makes me look up
and leap on my street
and examine every last one
of the leaves on the trees throwing
pure shade on me, here
where I often wait
for my friend to come gliding up
and take me away for latte and talk
to the café with the funny name
that may be gone next year—
but what year was it
that a man could know
what came next?
I plan to live now,
in a world kind enough
to wait for me; it didn't
just drop away when I no longer
noticed its effortless
passing through night
then day. It's my day
given me
by turning this morning
to catch the scent of grass;
I had to stop
because that quick little me
I didn't know was gone
returned, rushing chest and limbs
so I walk up the alley,
past the house where the sad woman lives,
past the man cursing under his car,
and past the children properly suspicious

when I kick
their soccer ball, past the couple
who toss their lives about, I'm out
the alley and onto the street and into
the bus with its load
of fellow-feeling—and look, here,
still one seat for me.

CALLING CHILDREN

I called my children
out of the garden.
I stood by the open car door,
my plaintive *c'mon*
c'mon full of doubt
about the success of the soft tone.

I determined, later as well,
how best not to connect
to events in the past
that overwhelmed me then.
(I do not
supply examples.)

I expect to leap one of these days
one way or the other into
one phase or another
through the brilliant sun
or more likely up against the moon.

I wonder what time it really is.
I have felt fire in me
and I have seen it burn
in my children as if a star
entered them one night
with a message
about their entire goodness.

I offer them bones
from my bones
but their view of the road,
grove, lake, blue hills,
white mountains
arises within.

A STORY

After six months I put the ring
back on and found once again
that it fit, that it could pass over
the fat part of the finger
and rest comfortably next to
the palm with its criss-cross
of lines someone other than me
might read to discover my destiny.
It's shining there now, a thing
of good gold, and when I ponder
past and future, I fiddle it round
and my eye can catch its gleaming
edge. So perhaps after all I did

lose weight although I still feel
winded running behind my plans,
and when I stand naked after bath
with that body in full light,
I see where life has packed itself on
in every minute of overtime—
and now I've added this ring,
a few ounces to lighten up
the hand. You did notice

right away, and asked why,
and right away I said
the ring no longer grips tight
but almost the way it felt
when a simple adornment on the left
could announce a change had come
into the world and here was its
symbol: continuity of the finest stuff,
not something we might hammer
out one night.

So after these months of ours
I find a form that fits, new now
as continuing to live
after a birth or death is new.
Whichever it is, I often pause
to think. But my hands refuse
change, want still to gather in flesh
which then must be released back to you
so you can fight my need
—hard at work in me—
to forge around you a circle
of my old ways, not exactly
that fabulous place where gold
is broken and mended seamlessly
or produced out of substance far more
fragile than straw.

PART II

HOW I JOINED HUMANITY AT LAST

When love
in the heart speaking to me
dies out, I walk
the street to be near
men and women who might recognize
the death in me.

Instead I see the death in them:
in that man's eyes a wound
glows through; this woman
loved a man
whose body turned away.
They could make no deal
to sidestep pain for the sake of
a good night's sleep, for
comfort and companionship
so regret
will not cut so deeply in years ahead
that it might kill.

I look for signs: a scrap of paper
on the street, the word
that will start me off again.
Instead I see
those I did not see before
who want from me
what none of us can give.
We turn away, and later
can only bear a very little violence
on TV, and later still,
awakened in our beds
with nothing but the clock to say
time has not yet passed,
our hearts turn

terrorist, aflame
in the two a.m. nightmare
with its need for vengeance
—and its sword of dismay.

WHAT COMES AFTER LOVE

—the self crying out
for its own
laundry hamper—no
silk mixed with sweats
wrapped up, shoved down
and lost—
        until one day
              he falls

                  in

through stink, a zipper
cutting his cheek: he's trapped
and who's out there but the cat?
Into the machine he'll go
to shrink unsorted
flattened by the spin and hanging now
limp.
            Time to think:
my mother, hell, did a lifetime
of laundry, mostly for boys,
it couldn't have been pretty
but it didn't diminish her.
When she went into the south bedroom
with my father, their sheets
sprang from the wind
rippling the outside line.
She came to complain eventually
of winter
and a husband
who was falling away;
never about the mitts
she made, then mended
and saved in a bag, washed wool

resurrected later
when love wasn't always there,
her hands still strong enough
to keep her mind from flying.

Every year she shrank—
why, I don't know—but I know
I need some of their clean
early love out of which
I dropped down
in the mud by the culvert.
I would write my name over and over,
unable to divide myself
from a father heading for wheat,
a mother back by the door
he went through.

THE EXHAUSTED PAST

Where did you go wrong
that you ended up
with this worthless life?
You could say anything here,
and it would not matter.

The exhausted past
tires you, so don't mumble on,
except to say you have read as many books
as the maple has leaves,
now flaring yellow into red
as if even the tree wishes to make
a clean break—and when it stands
in the winter wind and rain,
is that perhaps the necessary triumph
admitting spring?
Organic images! Soon each word
inside your books begins to assume
the shape of hope, the position
of the bean before it sprouts and curls upward
into the sky through thick
and thin and into clouds, a good place
to jump from,

glide down from—
wings appearing just as you need them
to make yourself renew again
what the years before
did to you, how they
reduced you to a crouch,
which you fall away from
even as the river rises to meet first your hands
held together in the piercing position of prayer
and then your lips, your streaming hair,
the one shoe that stayed with you.

THINKING MY NEIGHBOUR'S THOUGHTS

One day I stepped out
of my apartment and walked
down the hall to the entrance
and passed a brown door not unlike
my own; it, too, had a spy hole
through which I could have seen nothing
had I ventured to look in;
its numbers although different
from my own were yet near enough
to be almost mine.
As I passed by
I heard the noise, unmistakable
in its holding back and wrenching out,
of sobbing, and I froze there
and imagined the head tipped back,
the hands covering the face,
the mouth twisted—
and then I went on my way.

I have never seen
in these many months
the face behind that door,
I have never seen
who authored that anguish
on the day I was free to pass
and go outside into the unexpected
blue daylight of a winter sky.
Part of me simply went on,
stepping out to catch the air
on my cheeks and lips,
testing the whiteness of the street
with my soles to see
if I might glide
in my greeting of the day.

And part of me watched
everything I did, each step and sniff,
each thought of step and sniff,
and this part remembered
back to the room and door
behind which another watcher
crumpled on the couch.
This part scouted ahead
of the sun and breeze
and knew where I would pass
later in the day, near to evening,
and the question would be
not whether I would knock or pry
but rather how to say
(to him or her who lived within)
that beyond the thing wrung out of us
and the thought of the thing
and the observation of the thing,
frost has melted on the street,
and a great circle of flame
has been close at hand all day.

ENDHOME

You want to kill yourself,
but you have no place to do it.
You can't mess up the house:
unfair to those who live there.
You wish the government would fund
Endhome, a common place for those who need
a legal way to die.
There're abortion clinics, there're hospitals,
but for you and your kind, there's only
the river or the bridge or the fast car
over the edge and into the air.
You don't want that, do you?

"Come to Endhome," the jingle goes,
"those who are laden and those who are
weak and cannot be strong.
We have government-inspected,
government-tested ways
to help you achieve the great peace."

You want to end yourself
and still be somewhere, watching
what the world will do with your absence.
You'll sleep through the grief part
since the faces of those you love
will be hard, and if you were suddenly alive
they would kill you in their anger.
This is not a part to enjoy or contemplate much
even from the position of being very dead.
After the rush has swept by you
and the web of lives re-entangled itself,
then maybe you could peek out of your place
and marvel a bit at the change in the children.
But what of this world would you feel

if one of them, one night,
went through the doors of Endhome
looking for you?

REASONS FOR LIVING

... start with my children,
the way they carry air
into my rooms and make the windows
want to fly open
so the dining-room
daffodils raise their bent necks
and open their faces, speechless but full.
But no child can keep me
from my thinking
and I try the earth itself,
the smell of the green ravine,
the ruby-crowned kinglet
dancing in the buds of the conifers,
his wings never still,
until one evening he says to me,
"What's the matter with you?
Isn't it enough that I'm here?
You want to be me, is that it?
You want transformation?"
He's gone, and when I take a plant, later,
from the ravine, bring it here
into my life, I know
it can offer
only green and nothing more
when the light goes out.
But for the time I bend
in sweat and gently tear it
up from its world,
I have no thought,
I do not see myself,
I fill myself fully to the edges.
I know the edges are beginning
to fray, one hole already big enough
to fly a blackbird through,

slip a hand through, not mine
for they are busy grubbing,
but it could be a hand
of a lover I once had,
or a child that has grown while I slept.

FIRST RAIN, THEN SNOW

The spirit moves in the moment,
not in the hour.
In the sudden flick of flesh,
turn of phrase, a raised hand,
you are separated
from your previous life—and still you say
"Everything's fine."
Except one thing is not fine:
you forget to love your spouse one day and
it stretches into three, or at work
someone in your department tightens his grip
until you turn your face
to a new direction;

and by consigning yourself away from the world,
by saying no to those who cross your door
with the intention of demeaning you
because you have not held the proper theory
or sought after their truth,
you cut their power, you stop the fight.
You have been given this moment
not to speak aloud
but to say to yourself
what you want from life.

Now, lying on the bed, you see
out the window the tops of three trees
and with these you measure
first rain, then snow, then rain again,
then light, then dark, then leaves,
then wind. None of these
encroach on you or appear to make you
less than you are; neither do they
help much when you turn to your pillow

or rise, understanding that
the children's voices downstairs will eventually
call up to you.

YOU ARE BRAVE

Every day you are brave,
but today as the sun rose
one of your fingers died.
Just a bit of you (on the hand
you use for reaching out
in that half-conscious way
to grab and grind berries
under your nose); the end
went white and then all of it
stopped sending pleasure or pain,
sending nothing
until the idea came to you
from across the world
that part of you was dead.

What else—you begin to panic—
might also have departed?
Should you go to the doctor?
Modern medicine knows little
about the will. Go anyway
and receive the preparations
intended to revive;
but don't expect to capture back
that dear dead finger,
the one the children call
Tall One, his shadow large
upon the bedroom wall.
What do we call him now?
Sad One, the one who saw above
the crowd of stubby pink collaborators
but could find nothing to see?

You were right to imagine that twinges
running down to kiss the left wrist

have already decided to pull from you
the power of touch. Every day
you brave these small signs
and force yourself still to believe
the last light of the evening
will fall into your hands in a burst
before dark.

THE WAY PAST WORDS

Under the hands of the massage therapist
I begin to let go
of my old life
lodged in flesh.
Sadness arises out of my back and neck
and enters my thinking
without words. Then I
leave behind that soft flannel
table where for a moment
I was new, my throat working.
I walk where young men
bend their bodies for tools,
and I stop to imagine
who will fill the spaces
they are building. I see
a man who ponders his books,
feels fine in his work
and in the company of others, but then
his own conversations tell him
not to bother, he will not find
the way past words
into undivided being.
Two blocks later
I come to rest again
at the bottom of my voice,
in the grip of the words
most fundamentally mine.
So I turn back and
ask for her firmest hand
to reach through the sinews
and find what once served well;
once, but no more. Her hand
meets resistance; inch by inch,
deal-making, she pulls

from my chest this
child, a gnome grinning
as if he is seeing
the sun beyond death.
We watch as he speaks
and begins to age.
If she returns him to me
through the power of her hands
—pressing him back through my spine—
will I become suddenly
myself in the space between peace
and the word for peace?
Or fall instead into the heart
pounding for all that is nameless?

THE LOST OCEAN

A woman is heaving something
out of herself; an old man
leaves to float elsewhere
in a surprising turn of events.
From the speeding train you see
their hospital is the size
you could pick with your fingers
and take to your daughter,
patients permanently stilled,
stretched on beds,
tangled by tubes, bars,
stiff linen, the bland
morning meal, sun-washed sky
out beyond the nurse's
ever-cheerful plunge, smells
intended to mask other smells.

You came this far
not for the mountains but for
the scent of the sea,
and travelling each day since,
you hope to reach the ocean
you once lost: the great salt bath
speaks of life before and life to be.
Instead you fall and come to rest
staring at the beige blocks of a ward,
herded by events into that box,
your face no longer your own.

If some morning you cut flesh there,
and the mirror says the surge of blood
is just the mask you wear, then
feel all the restless cells!
The ones eager to return

spilling down and around—
and those others (you are told later
by a man in black and white
bending by your bed) always dart up
and can only be gathered by angels,
rough hands that they have, working overtime
to pick up the best part of you
they alone can see.

MY GOODNESS

Goodness is killing me, keeping me
far from my true self
which wants to be bad, so bad,
so very bad I will be marked with
a special letter—"B"—and everyone
will see and recognize in me
the man who came back from the good.

I am good to the people who left me
and good to the cat who didn't care;
she cares only for her bowl
at four. I am good to my car,
good to my colleagues, and good
to my waistline of fat. But I know
my life is not a good thing

to inflict on consciousness
or on my friends, to whom
I can only offer a cliché—of the good
old broken heart, which is really
not the heart at all for of course
it takes in blood and pumps it out
still. What is busted is the will, that

state of mind that decides what
works and what does not. Imagine
you can only see others better
than yourself; you are always less good
than the man up ahead, the tall one
with the pretty child on his shoulders.
All his good will pours out of him

into his child, neither of them
aware of that flow—for that

is what goodness really is, unconscious
sweetness given as breath, whereas
my gifts are always checked off,
another fair ornament to wear.
I cover myself with these bright devices

so no one can see what I've come to be:
the man whose borders have been sealed;
no one gets in, no one breaks out.
And inside, his quick whip
gets what he needs from all those
soft lovers of civility:
praise, assuredness. His goodness, yes,

gets him through the day, past
the landlady with her broom; allows him
to comment merrily on the sun,
exchange money for goods
—but at night he lies down
with his own heart all over again,
that dark witch he cannot change

or master, cannot evict
or overrule for she has pushed
at all the walls day and night
until she is looking from his eyes.
You can only see her in certain lights
or in the presence of certain words
spoken in the right way

and if you are good you cannot
see her at all. She will not be
revealed to those who cannot know
what she carries, what she grows

in her fine garden, those vines
I have learned to climb, the ones
that root and go down

into a self-soured soil
where the flowers of others
never grow no matter how
lovingly planted; and where night air
is all the air, damp on the skin
and in the hair, and its touch
recalls you to the first time

you stepped away from reason,
or the time love fled past you.

CLAUSTROPHOBIC

This is the day when your face
is tight although your lower lip
hangs in the morning unable to find
a word: around your heart
gather the clichés you could
dig into with your hands—look at them
working on their own,
left/right sentinels that so often
feel the world first while your lungs
send messages through correct channels,
reducing the world's body
down to the dazzling poverty of the physical you.

You climb city stairs,
marvel at your clacking bones.
Is there a quick way to go
through the world, out its door and into
another? Is there any way
an ordinary you can make a break?
Not the breaking of little bones
where pain burns you
deeper and deeper in,
but the tearing aside of ribs
to let out the sound of tissues talking,
words you speak
when you are laid out
for inspection
by those to whom you have released
your most final dreams:

that some day you will be free
from mess, from flesh,
the morning's routine of ritual
rearranging; that the powerful

parts of the day will be forged
not on the phone or by eye contact
but by blood-hammers;
that your time on earth is the end of time:
ancestors gone, cities levelled,
new towers built
and destroyed beyond comprehension
as you lift your hand up
as you push your hand down
in little shocks of ecstasy.

ONCE AGAIN AMONG THE HUMANS

It is so simple a need: to feel
God stirring once again among the humans,
in the cleverness, the capacities,
along the eyebrows and out through the prickle
of the skin—to be drenched
in God as you are sometimes
caught in a downpour and find yourself
not running for the old doorway
but stopping to be washed,
the umbrella down on the ground and the cold
dividing the hair on your head.

Flesh itself can take you
places, but you return to gnaw
on broken, unreleased, unreleasable matter,
the gloom you always feel
when you only want to feel
something more than your own machine.
Where else can you look? We've given up
flowers, our lovers' bodies, the descant
of the monk's chant: these sweet connectors
thrilled in the blood and mind

but what you seek is
not a murmur or a word,
not a vowel, not a breath
entering or shuddering out, nothing less
than union
beyond pain, weariness, sex, irony,
beyond mystery to inertia of the sort
a child will use to imagine
angels are watching and from time to time
interfering, causing cars to veer away from
a precious pet now out prowling

among the darkening, gold-flecked streets
you suddenly find yourself hurrying along
watching for an entrance.

ON THE PATH OF INNER DEVELOPMENT

There would have to be trees,
and in the trees, birds, but
first the trees: great cages of light
which shake down
some peace in those moments
I stray away from the needs
of the animals and the children
to lean like a schoolboy
and gaze nowhere but up
through a river of light, triggering
on that leaf, the way it signals
and routes sun out of heaven and straight
onto the back of my hand
before I am snatched away by a greater
blast of light, this one opening
past the big branch just above me
and going up so high I shift away
for fear I might fall off the ground
and into the air and turn and turn
and vanish and touch the last green thing
with my outstretched hand and find myself
going into the sound of my own A-a-ah—

The birds' giddy witnessing
I see first in my usual way.
As little ones, sparrows or finches,
they hurry each other
in among the leaves, and this
hustle draws me out of myself
and I discover my surprise
in their flashes of colour, the sharpness
of the eye in the one who hovers down close,
the sparkle of the beak,
the power of the crest—and I remember

out of nowhere the night bird
who comes so often to me of late, crying
just as I turn to sleep
its call of two notes
so like my own name, until I feel
my body wants to move, throw back the covers
and run to the window and see.

But now, here, under the tree
wings return to their grey shapes
and I stand up into mine
so the blood slides into action
and I continue making my way
out from under delight into the sun
until wind blurs that point
on the horizon I once thought
I had to reach but which now seems no more
than someone's idea of the place to begin.

DOWN IN THE VALLEY

When I return to the valley
it has changed—more houses
on the benches and clotheslines
through the forest, .
certain neighbours gone for good—
but I have changed more, my aging
more rapid than the hills.
The sky is low, suggesting
not rain or storm
but end of summer: I panic
slightly at the speed
and, knowing my own signs well,
take to the road that loops
pleasantly back upon itself.
I set out briskly, wave my arms
to shake off a mood engendered
by brooding hills, grey-belly
clouds and half-lit farms.
Too late to check myself,
I forget to see, fall into
self-analysis obsessively,
then haul myself back
to consider actual poplars rattling
beyond a fence, wonder there
if one leaf might shake
exactly as any other
on the tree. I myself vibrate
differently from other folk
although one or two
might hear my sound and be
attracted to its pitch. I play
a game to keep my hope intact:
by the time I reach the creek
I will be happy, or failing that

will drink from the water
and be made happy. I feel the liquid
flow out of my hand as I lift it
into my mouth, imagining
no difference between what
went into me and what goes
through the meadow where horses
flick, stamp, look my way,
then turn to see someone
coming up the road. I am surprised:
roads here are seldom
walked but rather driven on
by trucks with dogs wind-blown
in the back. I see a man
older than me, leathery, more bent.
I play a game: try not to say hello
to see what else might speak.
He plays, too, pushes back his cap
so I can see his forehead
damp with the upward climb
he's been achieving,
his eyes bright, his forearms
burnt gold. He passes by, boots
silent on the stones flung
to the side of the road.
I wish immediately
I'd called out some silliness
about the weather's
strange ways this year.
By the last bend I believe
had I more than nodded, had I
spoke, I could have transferred
onto him some of my day's
dim weight, which he

being sturdy would drop
into the hilltop's fringe of
ragweed and whirling dust.

NEXT LIFE

He will enter his next life
unencumbered—without person
or personality—and look out from nothing
and see what is and not think
it will serve him.
He will live under a bridge
and walk without one hammer
to make him stoop.
No strongmen will shout
across a shed from victims
who push and shove.
Just a fertile flood plain
upon which he will spread seed,
crops he will of course
not need to harvest or eat,
now being merely
a viewpoint of purified watching.

This life he engages
person by person. If a crony
withdraws from him and sends out
a tight heart
he must out-manoeuvre,
he calls the body and blood
of a Roman soldier
into himself and hollers
for infantry: they reach a river
where shadows of men dance
and call to trees,
and he grips his sword more tightly
to keep his arm alive
for soon he is running
to cut flesh
away from its life until he himself

wants only to fall on the ground
and pray that his children
will not be born
so far from the sea
that they may need
the old blood turbulence
of families, tribes,
to get themselves free.

HIS MOTHER'S FACE

Evening smells of snow
as a child—boy—
cuts through the shadows and bush;
far off, a neighbour's yellow beast
barks—it will come again
to attack his own dog,
fangs lunging into fur
while he shouts for them to stop.
Here the air released from the ground
rises up to touch his cuffs.
He has hunted too long
for the nest of the waxwing,
and now the dark has come
and the light of his heart is dim.

She will be wiping dishes,
she will be mending,
and she will look up
(later he will see this)
and send the ache into him
that says he is good
only if he gets away from dirt
seeping into the house, from the weaker
animals; and she imagines the city
with velour curtains
in tall rooms and the sounds
of men through the walls.

The next day he runs with his brace
of revolvers,
then comes slowly upon the house,
recalls his legs dangling down,
her shoulder sharp, and his head
no longer finding its place

in the softness
of her throat. Thus the child
comes home one day
changed, draws grief on his mother's face
as easily as he scars the white trees.

TRIP AWAY FROM HOME

His mouth wrenches down,
his head wags in disbelief
at this minor grief he's throwing
on his kids—a father given to tears
at farewells—and soon
the youngest is blubbering, too.
The oldest takes a stern line
and runs its straight across her mouth.
She's learned to hold down love,
as he had, until this unexpected
birth of softness rearranges
his insides so fast
he cannot check his heart
and falls instead—is felled—
against a bosom and is held
in bafflement.

He recalls
a beer-soaked table, a boy
jostled into roughness
who won't melt among men
untouched by brotherhood.
Thus wariness carried him
until an age
better to be through than in,
where the accumulation of losses
reaches a critical mass one day

as I believe it does

as it did for my father
who turned sorrow into a field
of blue flax
so it grew to rival

the sky itself: a lake
among the dust
                    at its edges
sullen men thrash and fold,
hands reach for stems and stalks
to test against their teeth.
I keep running past these hounds;
they gather around forks
flung into soft ground
to talk of nothing I can understand,
love shining in their eyes for the land
but not for one another
or for me.

POUCHES

To live in a time when men had pouches:
to be a monk in a brown wool robe
balanced on a bridge that crosses
a torrent, no rails but a rope
on the left, his right hand free
to clutch his pouch, a leather bag
rubbed shiny from use, a tight
string holds the little precious
objects of his time: coin
and bones of a saint
to greet the devil snaking
on every trail in and beyond
the walls of any town. At night
he worries his fire alive
again and again until struck down
at last by all the fearful words
that run through his head
he fingers his pouch one last time
and sleeps. Awakes years and years
later to haul his briefcase
out the door, banging it
on the fender of his Honda,
opens it upon his
altar-high display of paper,
programs, pens, photos
of offspring already out of date,
no leather in sight, crosses
not upon the wall but in the books,
the only pouch in his jeans,
which women streaming
past his door estimate, sensing
in this new arrival some antique scent
of wool and wet bark in the hair
and maybe in his grin the free gift

that arises whenever a body
knows longing is no sin.

SELF-ADMONITIONS

Not to set up structures
that require completion;
not to imagine the stronger light
of April, May, June, July
signals growth in him;
not to expect the earth to come roaring.
Still he is caught
unable to make the clean-and-jerk
required by the day, weak
in a human way
one time too many,
friends noting his grump and sag,
the announcement of decline
in the clutch of the night sheets
on his skin; but also this:
how to extend the head down
so the neck cracks, energy
flows into his legs
and he walks smiling into work.

Once he hankered for fall's
dark and glory, and the last days
in the race for silent white.
As a child he looked out
for the morning when, in the night,
the snow had arrived to present
the chance for tracks
criss-crossing into paths
that signalled where he's been
and continues to be going.

This spring takes on
direction: one more release
up into the light,

the colour of heat to come,
and ground good to lie on.
Not to linger there counting
blades of grass; not imagining either
how clouds break and drift—
and if they meet again
in this country—but to divine
in the scatter of the insect air
new wings approaching.

THE MOUSE AND MY MOTHER

The mouse in the house
reminds me my mother now
long dead fled
her black hair flying from snakes
who themselves chased mice
for food so they could continue
to chase. The mouse here
caught in a live trap
is taken outside, its head
large on its body, its eye
large in its head, safe
now to find other houses
and begin its tiny noises in the night
—or perhaps return to us
as I feel some days my mother
returns to me: after weeks
when I haven't considered her
suddenly I feel her close
not scrabbling in the walls
or dashing past my foot but gentler
in her announcement, a rocking
at the base of thought, a nosy
poking friendliness as if she
happened to be passing by and felt
the need to drift my way
for surely if she *is*
then how big a place she must be in,
big as the house is big
to that little one who finds us
sleeping and cuts along the walls
in search of crumbs
or the soft material out of which
a nest is built and filled
and more and more is pulled
out of nothing into form.

SMOKE

The man in apartment #1 fell asleep
after drinking, and his cigarette
fell, too, onto his bed
where the mattress embraced it
and began to smoke on its own.
I'd been dreaming: land, running water,
a deep well, cool mornings,
air from the mountain peak
rolling to the back door,
black bears lured
by bacon in my smoke.
I was dreaming of a journey,
sea-spume on my sandals,
wind under my hat when I reached port,
wharves heaped with colours,
tight lanes full of women
bending over charcoal fires
to feed small blackened faces.
I am dreaming the great hunter
leading a caravan of horses, dogs,
is me, out to find the child
seized by raiders and left to starve
on the spreading steppes
under a large rock frequented
by snakes in summer, wolves
in winter; on the fourth day
smoke stinging my eyes, I spy
a button from the child's vest
rolled among the many stones its size
—even our splendid native trackers
missed this sign—our horses
rear in the blue smoke, ready
for the last day's ride. I am dreaming
I am no longer dreaming, this is now,

the truth of daily living,
upon our backs
tiny bundles of memories
as we flee, night closing in
on the camps under the peak
of a white mountain, ravens in the trees
awaiting the half scraps
from the loosening hand of a child
who rolls close to his mother,
his wool coat catching the sparks
his father prods from the flame,
the man unable to sleep
on this hard ground
until he has drained down
the last of the red wine he carried
from his home.

PART III

THE BEAUTIFUL VOICE OF THE UNDERTAKER

... rises from the last pew
to help carry the frail body
of the old woman
away from her family, his tenor
carrying over us all, not
showing off or even showing the way

and those of us not caught up in
the moment as it flashes
and is gone
could tell
he has sung this song
before, and yet he sings also

for this woman,
to the soul which he could only
have known from her body,
and because his voice is strong
we can suppose—can we not—
he feels grief.

Now as he straightens his back
and opens his heart to the hymn
his own mother
fills the kitchen
with the sweet lift of soprano
on a Saturday afternoon when he himself

was too tired
to break out the games
or find his companions at the edge
of the woods, and so he sat there
in his own dreamy life,
and the cinnamon buns

and the warm milk in the jar
held him still and made him think
and when he asked her
she turned and was not fast
like sometimes she could be:
you will be a violinist one day,

—and he took that and changed it
to the man who blew the strong
sad notes at the end of the movie,
he would be the one who made tears,
and even then he could not understand
why sadness should be a desire

—and so he came to sing at funerals
not in any showy way
but as a voice we could follow
when he carried sorrow out the door into
the woods and laid it down
among the roots and leaves.

THE TRUE IMAGINED LIFE OF MY NEIGHBOUR

The old woman lies in her bed
and listens to the love cries
of her neighbours upstairs.
She can't imagine
any longer the preliminaries
to such an event—would they include

some teasing or anger
or just the knowledge
that today these two
were going to meet
in bed? She hears the rhythm
above her

and then she falls asleep.
Her other neighbour
is me, and I wonder
how far I might have to reach
beyond the boiled bone
and the tam

to find physical love in her.
She's dreaming now
and what dark rabbits
might she be chasing,
what souls are coming
to visit our block tonight?

She settled for
living in a building
without insects.
Different from those years
she had children
and together they lived

different from those
later years she had
nightmares of thrashing fury
because each of her kids
had failed her
even when she knew

they had not (in fact
they made adulthood).
We all had that mother
some of the time, when she
wanted to eat her young
and it was time for us to run,

her daughters perhaps
the most fearful of all,
until they reached time
apparently set aside
for the sanctioning of
abandonment, where

we find her today,
where we slip
and begin to feel the fall
from heaven
as a personal fall
and begin to think and eventually pray.

THE OLDER MAN

... walks through his streets,
looks in windows
in the early evening light. We know
he does not leave the sidewalk
yet he can talk about
the lives he sees: the white shirt

hung in the doorway,
or pictures
crowded in the hall.
Blurry figures
working with hands
—too distant to see

what might be knives, what
vegetable. The older man
looks over the city
and knows all the love in the world
and for the world
is starting to set

is going down,
leaving red lines
in its path.
Some say a big burst,
some, a green ray.
He says nothing to our versions

of how we live
if we look only at those
who seem to know
what is going on
and have helped to make it be.
He checks a moment

on himself
to see who is thinking now,
which older man:
the one with
the connotation—smarter
maybe but swinging down

—or the round guy in 203
with the sun in his face.
We see them warm afternoons
walking away from one another
as if neither noticed.
Our eyes are like that:

trained to notice minute changes
in common spaces,
who comes and goes, who stays
and where—and then we forget
all of it, and it sinks
into our souls

and we urge the old men on
to walk our streets,
not exactly spies, yet both
have seen the eye of the child
made sad
by the flesh of the mother

and the hand of the father,
by what is lost
and what is upright,
what flickers and is gone.
Our men walk and walk
and then recoil:

one to peer from a city window,
geraniums at his back,
until the angel of the hour
finds him and pierces his intentions
and releases him
from his unclear desire to be free.

The other? He escapes our attention
to walk the industrial shore
and attract the wild dogs
that live in the sea, their white tongues
licking his hand and tugging
his sleeve

into the salt—he bends to pat
their pretty heads
and call their names
and they come to him,
eager some days to be strong,
and some days sated and ready for rest.

THE MAN WHO INVENTED THE TURN SIGNAL

The man who invented the turn signal
walks out the factory gates
somewhere in the west
knowing he's done a service
to the world hitting the road
by telling the car behind

it's turning; we speak
as if the car has brains and eyes
—and the man who invented the turn signal
knows he should just listen to
the meadowlarks
now he's out the gates

but his mind keeps
going on, turning over
itself in all the corners
in order to make the signal
come back to neutral
on its own.

Already he has foreseen
a young woman driving a convertible—
she forgets to pull her signal off
so forever after she is turning
and all the cars behind her,
all the young men who follow her

go off in directions she isn't going,
she just keeps looking straight ahead.
Our man imagines that woman needs
him, wants his arm to reach over
and gently flick the signal back
and maybe she smiles

or thanks him
with her eyes, the blue
he'll wake up to some day, some place
he'd fix up for her, not
the bungalow he's in now,
he should be wealthy as can be:

he invented
the simple and worthwhile, so the future
won't give a thought to it,
he's already done that,
arriving at last
at that little rubber wheel

the bigger steering wheel rubs and
gently nudges back in place
with the brilliance of plain devising,
he could show her how it works,
draw her attention to his genius, then
gently drop his hand on hers,

so cool on the wheel even though
it was warm as sunny could be,
so much stretching out
between one meadowlark and another,
and the gift
of all those poles along the road, each one

saying *call me, you can call me,
if I've ever wanted to love a man
it would have to be someone like you,
someone who has brains and hands
like yours, good at signals
I can pick up along this road.*

This is the 1950s,
they come to love in a tender way;
everything that can happen
almost does. Best of all
their children are golden
from the sun.